YO-CAH-231

Dancing Lights in the Northern Sky

SRA

Columbus, OH

Front Cover © Pekka Sakki / epa / Corbis; **3** © European Space Agency / Photo Researchers, Inc.; **4-5** © Michael DeYoung / CORBIS; **7** © CORBIS; **8-9** © Reuters / CORBIS; **9** © Sally Bensusen / Photo Researchers, Inc.; **10-11** © Pekka Sakki / epa / Corbis; **12-13** © Dennis di Cicco / CORBIS; **14-15** © Hinrich Bîsemann / dpa / Corbis; **Back Cover** © Pekka Sakki / epa / Corbis.

SRAonline.com

 SRA

Copyright © 2008 by SRA/McGraw-Hill.

All rights reserved. No part of this publication may be reproduced or distributed in any form or by any means, or stored in a database or retrieval system, without the prior written consent of The McGraw-Hill Companies, Inc., including, but not limited to, network storage or transmission, or broadcast for distance learning.
An Open Court Curriculum.

Printed in China.

Send all inquiries to this address:
SRA/McGraw-Hill
4400 Easton Commons
Columbus, OH 43219

ISBN: 978-0-07-608761-7
MHID: 0-07-608761-1

2 3 4 5 6 7 8 9 NOR 13 12 11 10 09

The McGraw-Hill Companies

It's a cold, clear night. You step outside to breathe in the sharp winter air. You can see your breath in the chilly breeze. But the sight you see as you look up takes your breath away. In the northern sky, bands of green and greenish-blue lights shimmer and wave. Are you imagining this amazing sight? Is it a dream? No, you are viewing one of Earth's great wonders. They are the strange and beautiful Northern Lights.

The Northern Lights are an aurora. Auroras happen near Earth's poles. They appear high in the sky when solar particles hit Earth's atmosphere. Solar particles are bits of energy from the sun.

In the northern half of Earth, these lights appear near the North Pole. They are called *aurora borealis*. This means "northern lights." Lights that appear near the South Pole are called *aurora australis*, or "southern lights."

The Northern Lights have different forms and colors. They might look like curtains of light or bands across the sky. They also appear as patches of light or arcs shaped like rainbows. They seem to move and ripple as though a light wind were blowing them. The lights can be pale or bright. Sometimes they are so bright that they can be seen far away from the poles. The colors vary, depending on how and where the solar particles hit Earth's atmosphere.

In ancient times people lived
in awe of these dramatic lights.
They tried to explain the strange
lights with ideas and stories. They
believed that the Northern Lights
were signs of coming trouble. When
sickness came or crops failed, the
strange lights were often blamed.

Some thought that people who
became lost in the cold northern
places turned into dancing lights.
Others believed the lights could
come close enough to touch them.
They thought the lights might harm
them if that happened.

One story from Denmark tells
of swans that flew too far north.
They landed on water and became
trapped forever in the ice. The lights
move as the swans flap their wings
and reflect the sunlight.

Even now the Northern Lights
are a mystery in many ways. Still,
we have learned a lot. We know that
the Northern Lights don't warn of
coming danger. Instead they show
one way Earth is protected.

A nineteenth-century drawing of the Northern Lights

Solar flares

The Northern Lights begin with activity on the sun. The sun may seem steady and unchanging. But it is a very active star!

Sometimes sunspots appear on the surface of the sun. Sunspots are areas of strong magnetic action that can send bits of solar material flying. Solar winds blow out from the sun's surface. When this happens, powerful streams of energy shoot out into space. Some of them head straight toward Earth.

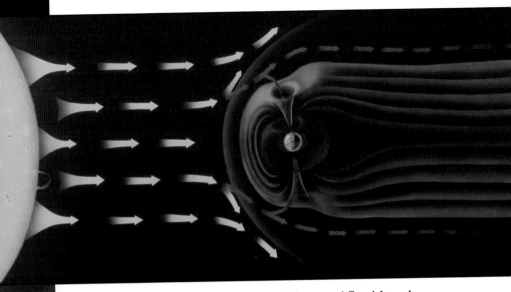

Particles from the sun are pulled toward Earth's poles.

These streams would be dangerous if they hit Earth's surface. They could hurt plants, animals, and people. This does not happen, though, because Earth's atmosphere offers protection.

Have you ever played with a bar magnet? Some metals are pulled toward the ends, or poles, of a magnet. Earth is a giant magnet. Particles from the sun are pulled toward the poles as they approach Earth. There the particles enter the upper levels of Earth's atmosphere.

The solar particles are traveling very fast when they reach Earth's atmosphere. There, they strike the atoms of many different gases. The impact from these tiny collisions creates light energy. When enough collisions occur at the same time, people can detect them as moving lights in the sky. In times when the sun is very active, more particles reach Earth. Then the Northern Lights become incredibly bright and even more beautiful.

The Northern Lights occur high in the sky. Most are more than sixty miles above Earth's surface. Different gases are found in the different layers of the atmosphere. Every type of gas gives off a different color. This is why the color of the Northern Lights varies as much as it does.

Red lights usually happen much higher in the atmosphere, where solar particles mix with oxygen. Purple-red lights occur when they mix with nitrogen closer to Earth. Scientists analyze the lights to learn where the collisions are happening.

The Northern Lights change as the weather on the sun changes. The sun is more active about every eleven years. At that time more of the sun's particles shoot toward Earth than usual. This makes the Northern Lights very bright.

The lights also become brighter about every twenty-five days. This is the length of time it takes for the sun to rotate on its axis. The Northern Lights are brighter when an active spot on the sun's surface faces Earth. The Lights dim as that spot rotates away.

The Northern Lights are usually most active in late autumn and early spring. They are brightest just before midnight. The best places to view them are in northern areas, such as Alaska and Canada. Near the poles, the lights might be seen on any clear night. During some especially rare and active years, the lights are visible much farther south. In 2001 they could be seen in nearly all parts of the United States.

The Northern Lights occur in an oval-shaped area around the North Pole. They are easiest to see very late in the evening, away from the bright lights of cities.

People who do not live near areas where the Northern Lights dance in the sky can still see the lights. Scientists have set up Web sites on which anyone can watch the Northern Lights as they happen.

People once believed that these dancing lights caused trouble. Now science has replaced those myths with facts. Scientists are trying to accumulate more information to help them better understand these beautiful lights. But one fact will never change. The Northern Lights will always fill people with awe.

These lights are a great reminder of how amazing Earth and this universe really are. Who knows? Maybe you will see them someday. And maybe they will lead you to scientific adventures of your own!

Vocabulary

solar (sō´ lər) (page 4) *adj*. Having to do with or coming from the sun.

awe (ô) (page 6) *n*. Great wonder, fear, and respect.

dramatic (drə ma´ tik) (page 6) *adj*. Exciting or interesting.

impact (im´ pakt´) (page 10) *n*. The force of one object striking against another.

detect (di tekt´) (page 10) *v*. To find out or notice; discover.

varies (vâr´ ēz) (page 10) A form of the verb **vary**: Changes; makes or becomes different.

analyze (an´ ə līz´) (page 11) *v*. To find out what something is made of by taking it apart.

accumulate (ə kyo͞om´ yə lāt´) (page 15) *v*. To gather or pile up.

Comprehension Focus: Classify and Categorize

1. At different times people thought the Northern Lights were caused by people turning into lights, by swans flapping their wings, and by solar particles hitting Earth. Classify these three ideas into the categories *Myth* and *Fact*.

2. Reread page 5. Name two categories into which the Northern Lights can be classified.